# HOME GROWN

# in the

# Haiku Garden

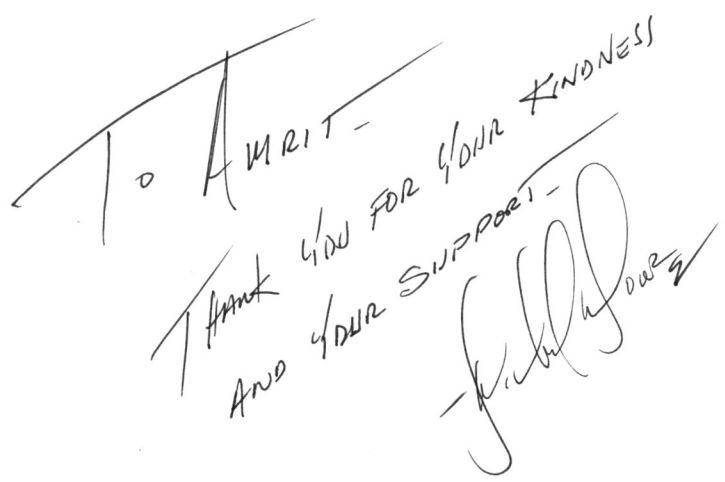

Mustard Seed
Press

**also by Michael Moore**

*Chocolate Haiku*
*Chocolate Chips*

**Cover by Martha K. Grant**

"My Garden Blooms at Midnight"
Acrylics on canvas

Copyright 1995 by Michael Moore
Library of Congress 595-304
All rights reserved. Printed in the
United States of America.

*1 2 3*

For Information on the Contemporary
Haiku in The Classroom, write to, P.O.
Box 681694, San Antonio, Tx., 78268-1694

# Contents

Acknowledgements

Introduction

| | |
|---|---|
| Flowers | 1 |
| Birds | 9 |
| Fish | 18 |
| Plants | 20 |
| Fruit | 22 |
| Trees | 24 |
| Animal Potpourri | 27 |
| Young & Old | 31 |
| Butterflies | 36 |
| Dragonflies | 38 |
| Small Wonders | 40 |
| Music | 44 |
| Clouds | 47 |

## Contents

| | |
|---|---|
| Mountains | 49 |
| Water | 51 |
| By The Way | 62 |
| Day | 65 |
| Night | 70 |
| Spring | 75 |
| Summer | 79 |
| Autumn | 81 |
| Winter | 85 |
| Snapshots | 89 |
| Reflections | 94 |

*Acknowledgements*

*Special thanks to Mary Moore, Celestine Shambrey, John & Donna Chevallier, Joseph O'neal and Ken Warfield.*

*To the tea group, thanks so such.*

*This book is dedicated to Oteka Moore, a gardener who tended rainbows of flora and fauna.*

# Introduction

*Home Grown in the Haiku Garden is written for the gardener in you. Whether you put your hands into the soil, explore a nature trail, send flowers, or have a salad, the garden touches your life.*

*The comtemporary haiku will be your guide as you tour the garden's landscape. This style of poetry combines Western free verse with the three line brevity of the Japanese haiku. It is the beauty in each style that gives the reader a unique view when the two styles are brought togather within each poem.*

*It is with great pleasure that I share with you Home Grown in the Haiku Garden.*

*Floating above*

*the pond's reflection*

*water lilies scent the morning breeze.*

Flowers 1

*Before the king*

*sits plum blossoms*

*mother of the butterfly.*


    *White gloves*

        *in the magnolia tree*

            *touched the summer breeze.*


*Hungry flowers*

*hunting butterflies*

*in a rain forest dream.*

*Flowers 2*

Tulips

playing catch

in the rain.


                Turning around

                once again

                to leave the cherry blossoms.


Plum blossoms

filling the air

with the blush of spring.

Flowers 3

Scent of jasmine

from the neighbor's yard

visits our water garden.


        Poppy field

        fluttering in the breeze

        butterflies in bloom.


Little flowers

painting landscapes

full of butterflies.

Flowers 4

*Exploring*

*the wall*

*roses falling over.*



*Sun's reflection*

*on a cloudy day*

*water lilies at heart.*



*Fresh violets*

*floating in a bowl*

*butterflies in the clouds.*

*Flowers 5*

Under cherry blossoms

on a far mountain

flowers painting landscapes.



Looking out

over the sea

cliffs of cherry blossoms.



Prehistoric flowers

wading in a vase

bird-of-paradise.

Flowers 6

Little clouds

floating by the trellis

white clematis in bloom.



Locked in winter

released by spring

plum blossoms bursting.



Sun setting

on the lilies

inhaling their reflection.

Sharing an evening

with fireflies

magnolias in the breeze.



Breath of jasmine

in the dead of night

blooming from the shadows.



Petals falling

over night

snapshots of the moon.

Flowers 8

Awakened at dawn

by hundreds

of chirping trees.



Cock crowing

just before sunrise

how enlightening.



Cranes glided

over the marsh

settling in the dew.

Birds 9

*Cardinal comet*

*blazing through the mist*

*following a song.*


*Two birds*

*making plans*

*one twig at a time.*


*A flock of geese*

*flew across the road*

*having the right of way.*

Birds 10

Returning birds

search for eaves

the barn no longer stands.




Geese talking

over my head

therefore I have nothing to say.




Summer hawk

floats on flute music

rising from the veranda.

Birds 11

*Blue Jays yelling*

*at their neighbor's again*

*I've never heard them whisper.*




*Fleeing hawk*

*no place to hide*

*among the angry crows.*




*Ducks dipping*

*tails in the air*

*a meal of tender shoots.*

Birds 12

The bird bath

quietly sunning itself

between showers.


Unbearable heat

sparrows with open mouths

praying for rain.


Hanging baskets

from a cliff

swallows nesting.

*Huge feathers*

*white on the lake*

*swans in plum-scented blossoms.*

    *Clouds of wings*

    *above the stream*

    *kingfisher hovering.*

*Wild geese*

*pay no attention*

*to my little pond.*

Birds 14

Red leaf
on a bare branch
January cardinal.




        Colorful daydream

        a cardinal on the bough

        warming the winter's chill.




Watering flowers
swallows flying by
taking little swallows.

Birds 15

*Water birds*

*feathered rainbows*

*descending from the sky.*


    *Hairy fruit*

    *on the plum tree*

    *bird's nest in late autumn.*


*Thin clouds*

*race across a greying sky*

*geese in autumn wind.*

Birds 16

*Nightingale's song*

*from distant pines*

*beckons the summer moon.*


*Night hawks fly*

*by the electric sun*

*one street lamp rising.*


*Fishing birds*

*dive in to the night*

*swallowing shimmering comets.*

Birds 17

*The fish*

*jumped in*

*the splash.*

 

*A rainbow of fish*

*among the coral*

*bathed in eternal rain.*

 

*Small mouth bass*

*biting the summer sky*

*clouds swimming away.*

Fish 18

*Fish swimming*

*in smaller circles*

*dry season on the Kalahari.*




*The goldfish*

*with sunspots swim*

*beneath the waterfall.*




*Darkening shadows*

*swallowed Mr. Trout*

*morning coughed him up.*

Fish 19

Field of straw hats

growing in summer

who will wear you in spring.




Weeds in my grass

how well you flower

with roots of iron will.




Wind brushed reeds

waving in the pond

stirring the sky's reflection.

Plants 20

*The summer hurricane*

*a charging wild boar*

*what's left of my vegetable garden?*


*Pond reeds growing*

*from shadowed depths*

*piercing reflections-casting them back.*


*Surf-fed tide pool*

*sea anemone's pond*

*flowers in a bowl.*

Plants 21

Strawberries ripen
far too slowly
for a youthful tongue.


    Scent of oranges
    captured the room
    holding roses hostage.


Over the fence
peach tree limb
bearing gifts.

Fruit 22

Into the night

go plums

with the stars.



        Out of the night

        come plums

        with the dawn.



In the porceline bowl

I placed purple plums

feasting on the contrast.

Fruit 23

*Perfect day*

*to fly a kite*

*willow leaves at play.*

*In the orchard*

*on the ground*

*apples rolling.*

*Thinning mist*

*on distant hills*

*autumn trees ablaze.*

Trees 24

*Falling*

*through the silence*

*an autumn leaf.*


*Such a bouquet*

*of leaves*

*arranged by an autumn whim.*


*Gently hurling*

*leaves to ground*

*autumn's gravity.*

*Plants 25*

*The withered tree*

*has character*

*written all over its trunk.*

*Sound of sea*

*so far from shore*

*waves in mountain pines.*

*Dead wood*

*passed out on the ground*

*helping mushrooms grow.*

Trees 26

*Jungle stalking*

*in jaguar's fur*

*painted flowers of prey.*

*Cat staring*

*in a liquid mirror*

*fish darting through the reflections.*

*Oh, so quick*

*lime green snake*

*forever grass and shadow.*

Animal Potrourri 27

Acrobatic squirrels

swing from limb to limb

through the walnut trees.

        Across the corner

        of my imagination

        shadow of a lizard.

That rustling sound

from the bushes

is bigger than a lizard.

Animal Potpourri 28

On the veranda

cat stretching

its shadow.



        Summer buds

        tiny tree frogs

        clinging to the reeds.



Caught the frog

that lectured last night

outside my bedroom window.

Animal Potpourri 29

Wild frog

tamed by innocence

staring at the children.




Cat sitting

on the shadow of a chair

comfortably napping.




In the neighbor's yard

white rabbit running

through the full moon shadows.

Aninal Potpourri 30

Children running

through cherry blossoms

their voices play hide and seek.




       Windmill child

           youngest son of the butterfly

           turning cartwheels in spring.




Children in butterflies

dancing as breezes play

melodies only they can hear.

YOUNG & OLD

Children running

along the river's edge

watch out Mr. Toad.




Painting summer

as a child

the sun was often yellow.




Children

chasing butterflies

all over spring.

Young & Old 32

*Angels laughing*

*in peach blossom skies*

*such joy from the children's swing.*

*My neighbor's wall*

*is no match*

*for kite or curious children.*

*Children looking*

*out at winter*

*through the eyes of spring.*

*Young & Old 33*

Captured

by mother's roses

my heart belongs to spring.




        Father's pipe

        for many years

        has been our weather vane.




Empty chair

mother is visiting friends

beyond the autumn leaves.

Young & Old 34

Saturday morning

cutting the grass

to cut the grass again.


    From now

    until next year

    I'll keep plum blossoms in mind.


Though snow is deep

a friend visits

with warm hands and soup.

Young & Old 35

*Butterfly*

*on the cold hibachi*

*wings ablaze.*


*Busy day*

*on the veranda*

*watching butterflies climbing trees.*


*Butterflies and flowers*

*came to the field*

*as their ancestors last spring.*

*Butterflies 36*

*When asked*

*about butterflies in dreams*

*she looked toward the cherry blossoms.*



*Butterfly traveling*

*across the afternoon*

*aboard a summer breeze.*



*Dandelion children*

*leaving home*

*to join the butterfly circus.*

*Butterflies 37*

At my feet

a slice of sky

bluest little dragonfly.



        Blue dragonflies

        on a clear day

        rise and become the sky.



Dragonfly sits

on a throne of reed

motionlessly dancing in the wind.

Dragonflies 38

On a reed
orange dragonfly
aflame.



    Skimming skies
    the dragon-flies
    above the garden pond.



Autumn wind
growing winter-like teeth
devouring butterflies.

Butterflies 39

Dusty thongs

at the front door

a cricket tries one on.

Spider's web

between the reeds

captures cherry blossoms.

Friends walking

just a step ahead

grasshoppers in summer grass.

Spider leaps

from a peach tree branch

ancient bunji jumper.




        The spider

        rebuilding

            after the spring rain.




From the edge

of my nap

crickets calling.

Small Wonders 41

*Humming*

*work songs*

*busy bees.*



*Busy bee*

*tumbles into a flower*

*departing all abuzz.*



*Grasshopper*

*upon the page*

*speed-reading.*

*Small Wonders 42*

Sun's reflection

in the shade

swallowtail butterfly.


This evening

cicadas singing

their old favorites.


Cicadas' song

grinding silence to dust

I await the nightingale's dew.

Through plum blossoms

a light mist

guides the temple bells.

 

The wind chime

fell in love with a spring breeze

oh how their children sing.

 

Nightingale's song

wrapped the evening

in splendor.

Music 44

*Rain forest singing*

*way into the night*

*in honor of an incredible moon.*


*Old gate's song*

*swings in autumn wind*

*my child knows its song by heart.*


*Bell's last toll*

*flies away with the geese*

*over the horizon.*

Music 45

Now that autumn has gone

I can see past cherry trees

and hear the temple bell.




        Wind chimes

           sing with doves in spring

           howling with the wolves in winter.




Temple bell rings

spring time blooms

in the winter snow.

Music 46

*Sunny day*

*rain is dry*

*no puddles for clouds to swim.*

 

*Daydreams in clouds*

*paint the sky*

*under cherry blossoms.*

 

*Clouds floating*

*between the lilies*

*in skies of blue and green.*

Clouds 47

Abandoned tea cup

on the patio

full of cloudy weather.


Clouds rolling

over the lake

water wheels in the sky.


Grey clouds

drawing a rainy curtain

across the meadow.

Clouds 48

Shedding snow

Mount Fuji

dresses for spring.




From the mountain

rocks tumbling

down into the clouds.




Occasionally

growing a tree

bonsai mountainside.

From the mountain

our village looks small

the mountain that fits in our window.




        Autumn's breath

        slowly makes its way

        down the maple mountain.




Out of the mountains

storm clouds marching

toward the family wind chimes.

Mountains 50

The glacier

weeping

it seems like forever.

Cold wave

roaring down the mountain

in tides of an avalanche.

New snow

only my eyes

visit neighbors today.

Water 51

*Frozen moments*

*pelt the earth*

*hail the lash of heaven.*




*Held hostage*

*by the hailstorm*

*for fear of a good beating.*




*High tide*

*winter storm*

*snow right up to the sky.*

Water 52

Snowy morning

all seems white

even the faint call of a crow.




        Frozen pond

        the frogs are taking

        their annual vacation.




Dreaming of spring

I reached for the gate

stumbling in the snow.

Water 53

Cupping hands

in clear water

spring rain fills the valley.




First fruit

before the cherry blossoms

sunlit dew on the bow.




Rainy day

no sparrow wing

to dry a watery sky.

Water 54

*Passing rain*

*chattering sparrows*

*bid it farewell.*


*Rain spilling*

*over the mountains*

*filling a barrow with clouds.*


*Rain drops*

*ring their way*

*around the pond.*

Water 55

Rain clouds

pouring reflections

on the desert floor.




Quiet stream

encountering stones

babbles like a brook.




Rising river

making its way

up the path to my door.

Water 56

*Drop by drop*

*water nibbling its way*

*along the rock.*

 

*Evening rain*

*falls upon the grass*

*smell of earth ascends.*

 

*Beyond freezing rain*

*I hear singing*

*last summer's nightingale.*

Water 57

*Little streams*

*of crystal waters*

*explore a steamy window.*


*Butterflies drift*

*in and out of my daydreams*

*watching snowflakes fly.*


*Tucked away*

*in the winter snow*

*spring rapids.*

Water 58

*Understanding gravity*

*rain drops fall*

*finding companions they water-fall.*


      *Water steps*

        *upon the stones*

      *in footprints of a waterfall.*


*The waterfall*

*singing a duet*

*with a frog.*

Water 59

*Waterfall*

*at the pond*

*sings a moving song.*

*The goldfish*

*with sun spots swim*

*beneath the waterfall.*

*Pond singing*

*as water falls*

*over night.*

Water 60

Sea anemone

in fresh waters

fireworks in celebration.


Day and night

wave after wave

moon, sea and tide.


The monsoon

wringing wet

came ashore.

Water 61

*Winding road*

*settles deep in the forest*

*beyond the curious eye.*


*Morning walk*

*on a well worn path*

*beside a nameless stream.*


*Resourceful path*

*at the stream*

*turned to stepping stones.*

By The Way 62

*Stepping stones*

*without reservation*

*crossed the stream.*

 

*A familiar path*

*winds through the forest*

*all alone.*

 

*The gardener placed*

*each stepping stone*

*in honor of serenity.*

By The Way 63

How reassuring

each step I take

upon His stepping stones.

    Stepping stones

    exploring the garden

    moistened by spring dew.

The garden path

encountered an old tree

and respectfully walked around it.

By The Way 64

*Chattering birds*

*have seen the light*

*dawn must be moments away.*

*Night and plum*

*go their separate ways*

*in the dawn.*

*Sunlit beads*

*of morning dew*

*adorn a spider's web.*

*Day 65*

*Right over*

*the fence*

*a sun rising.*

      *Morning light*

      *like a rooster's top*

      *zinnias crowing.*

*Glowing in the morning*

*dreaming landscapes*

*on a rice paper day.*

*Day 66*

Brilliant dream

in morning light

falling cherry blossoms.




Sunny afternoon

fish pond spawns

autumn leaves in koi.




Strips of color

above the lake

forest green, snow white and sky blue.

Day 67

*The afternoon*

*has a whimsical smile*

*squirrels playing on the hammock.*

*Shadows falling*

*on the old oak fence*

*in light of the afternoon.*

*The sun*

*this afternoon*

*shedding light on evening.*

*Day 68*

*Setting sun*

*wrapped in evening haze*

*muted golden landscape.*

*Sun going down*

*in the garden*

*jasmine rising with the moon.*

*Yoke of the sun*

*falls beyond the mountains*

*illuminating my dreams.*

Day 69

*Full moon*

sketches the garden

erased by the setting sun.

    *Evening walk*

    sky carries the lantern

    a beautiful summer moon.

*So moving*

a theater at play

fireflies come and go.

Night 70

*Hot petals*

*in the night sky*

*fireworks in bloom.*

*The summer night*

*wearing jewels*

*fireflies, stars and a moon.*

*Night*

*circles the bonfire*

*and leaps between the flames.*

*Night 71*

Through darkness

floats a view

of the nightingale.




4th of July

fireworks painting

neon palm trees.




Heavenly tides

coming and going

clouds passing over the moon.

Night 72

Shadows wander

day and night

resting beneath the new moon.




Moon rising

through the window

jasmine in full bloom.




Under stars

among chattering crickets

tranquil moonbeams.

Night 73

*By the sea*

*moon sweeping*

*tide in, tide out.*

*In the wind*

*a harvest moon*

*gathering leaves.*

*Swimming*

*up river*

*a salmon moon.*

Night 74

*Early spring*

*tulips brilliant*

*in the rain.*


*Spring in mask*

*of flower and leaf*

*butterflies in your hair.*


*Such companions*

*spring and flowers*

*playing leap frog hill and valley.*

*Spring 75*

From spring

in the village

we gather cherry blossoms.

      Spring wind

         grabbed my hat

           with hands I could not see.

Breath of spring

full of fish

north of the hibachi.

Spring 76

*Spring winds
carrying fragrant shadows
plum trees in bloom.*


*Each spring
fragrant snow
west of the cherry trees.*


*Spring cleaning
is far behind
petals everywhere.*

Spring 77

Little puddles
full of sky
after the spring rain.



Spring departs
from the window
in snows of cherry blossoms.



Spring passed
over the mountain
leaving frogs to sing.

Spring 78

Summer heat

steaming over the mountains

collecting morning dew.


Summer wind

arranging butterflies

in the meadow.


Lounge chair

in a shady spot

reclining.

Spring 79

Summer shadows

cross the patio

cooling my afternoon tea.




Summer evening

before the fireflies

a gentle rain clears the air.




At summer's end

the cuckoo calls

quietly for a change.

Summer 80

High hopes
for an Indian summer
flew away with the geese.



Summer leaves
no longer sun themselves
autumn wind has spoken.



The dust
from spring cleaning
returns as autumn haze.

Autumn 81

Harvest time

on valley floor

beneath the snow-filled alps.


Autumn day

silent cuckoo

leaves softly crashing.


The garden

wind in leaves

autumn theater at play.

Autumn 82

*At the gate*

*coming and going*

*autumn leaves.*


*Summer sun*

*burning bright*

*among the autumn leaves.*


*Late autumn skies*

*full of rain*

*smothering crimson leaves.*

Autumn 83

Autumn alone

with the cherry trees

my memories in full bloom.


This morning

first snowflake

of the year.


Lightning opens

the autumn darkness

leaving shadows to flower and die.

Autumn 84

*Winter storm*

*bit into the mountains*

*devouring my view of autumn.*


*Winter gale*

*pushed autumn aside*

*moving wind chimes to tears.*


*Winter morning*

*at the well*

*spring still buckets away.*

*Winter 85*

*Frosty morning*

*mist streaming*

*from every conversation.*


*Winter sun*

*growing shadows*

*in an empty planter.*


*New Year's Day*

*yet the cold*

*seems so familiar.*

*Winter 86*

*Softly snowing*

*winter's children*

*at play.*


*Winter gale*

*swelling tides*

*returning cliffs to the sea.*


*In the dead*

*of winter*

*a moon blossoms.*

*Winter 87*

*Sun dips*

*in an inkwell night*

*painting miles of new moon snow.*



*Light*

   *from a neighbor's home*

   *blinks its way through the snow.*



*At the end*

*of my blanket*

*winter's breath.*

*Winter 88*

Eager to travel

the melting snow

slips away to the river.


Rushing river

smoothing rough edges

slowly.


Just behind

a wave of geese

the tillers.

Snapshots 89

*Asleep*

*in the meadow*

*dreaming of landscapes.*



*Axe gnawing*

*deep in the forest*

*chopping holes in silence.*



*Mountain path*

*through the forest*

*adorned with butterflies.*

Snapshots 90

The mountain path

opens and closes

in the misty forest.




Lost

in the forest

looking for a familiar tree.




Mountain

growing a bonsai tree

on the side.

Snapshots 91

*From the ledge*

*boulders become pebbles*

*and the river a stream.*


*Spring evening*

*breezes painting*

*a fragrant collage.*


*Heron fishing*

*at river's edge*

*catching comets.*

*Snapshots 92*

*Parting trees*

*a road*

*coming and going.*

*In the dawn*

*night finds shelter*

*at the far side of the sky.*

*A stranger walking*

*on this nameless road*

*turns out to be my nieghbor.*

*Snapshots 93*

## Child's Play

Windmill child

youngest son of the butterfly

turning cartwheels in spring.

Painting summer

as a child

the sun was often yellow.

My child is running

along the river's edge

watch out Mr. Toad.

Reflections 94

*Birds*

*Cranes glided*
*over the marsh*
*settling in the dew.*

*Two birds*
*making plans*
*one twig at a time.*

*Fishing birds*
*dive into the night*
*swallowing shimmering comets.*

*Rain Forest Dream*

*Summer heat*

*steams over the mountains*

*collecting morning dew.*

*Water steps*

*upon the stones*

*in footprints of a waterfall.*

*Spider's web*

*between the reeds*

*captures a rainbow of blossoms.*

*Ducks dipping*

*their tails in the air*

*a meal of tender shoots.*

*Reflections 96*

*Floating logs*

*with bulging eyes*

*razor jaws are hunting.*

*Oh, so quick*

*lime green snake*

*forever grass and shadow.*

*Sun descends*

*as evening falls*

*before the fireflies.*

*Lily pads*

*floating in moonlight*

*immersed in jasmine breeze.*

Home Grown Haiku

Lamp light
upon the evening wall
old friends visit.

Red peppers
in our winter soup
a little taste of summer.

Desert a-la-mode
talking to friends
conversation ripe with plums.

After dinner
the cat
yawns with satisfaction.

Reflections 98

Wooden floors

waxed with light

staged the evening play.

A little baked clay

from the potter's wheel

beautifully held evening tea.

Miniature streams

of crystal waters

explored the steamy windows.

The moon and I

stayed up all night

staring at one another.


Reflections 99

*Tears falling*

*from the wind chimes*

*last day of winter.*

*Our scarecrow*

*impeccably dressed*

*in his tattered best.*

Reflections 101

*Butterfly path*

*floating through the forest*

*upon a fragrant breeze.*

*Quills drawing circles*

*in a robin's egg sky*

*calligraphy of the hawk.*

*Eagles soaring
above an ocean
of bluebonnets.*

*Bar-b-que*

*in the garden*

*mesquite among the roses.*

*Silhouette at sunset*

*evening in light*

*of the whipoorwill.*

Sundown

in the lantana

fireflies on the rise.

"Spring wind    grabbed my hat    with hands I could not see."
HARUKAZE NI      BÔSHI TSUKAMARE      MIENU TE DE
はるかぜに        ぼうし つかまれ        みえぬ 手で

"The moon and I    stayed up all night    staring at one another"
TSUKI TO WARE      MITSUMEATTE      YO O AKASHI
つき と われ        みつめあって      よ を あかし

**Translated by Kazuyo**